Nipsey Hussle on Entrepreneurship

Business and Money Lessons Inspired by Nipsey Hussle

With, Step by Step Checklist on How to Implement This into Your Life

By

JJ Vance

Table of Contents

Disclaimer and Note to Readers:

This is an unofficial tribute book to Nipsey Hussle from a fan, for a fan to support his legacy.

The information in this book has been provided for educational and entertainment purposes only.

The information contained in this book has been compiled from sources deemed reliable and it is accurate to the best of the Author's knowledge; however, the Author cannot guarantee its accuracy and validity and cannot be held liable for any errors or omissions.

The fact that an individual or organization is referred to in this document as a citation or source of information does not imply that the author or publisher endorses the information that the individual or organization provided. This is an unofficial fan tribute book and has not been approved or endorsed by the Nipsey Hussle or his associates.

Before You Go Any Further, Download Your Free Gift!

Thanks for checking out **"Nipsey Hussle on Entrepreneurship."** You have made a wise choice in picking up this book!

Because you're about to discover many interesting tidbits of Nipsey Hussle you never knew before!

But before you go any further, I'd like to offer you a free gift.

My Ultimate Collection of Links to Nipsey Hussle's YouTube Videos!

If you're a Nipsey fan, you'll DROOL over this!

<u>But I'll take it down if too many people claim it as it's my personal treasure</u>. Don't miss out!

Get it before it expires here:
http://bit.ly/nipseybonus

Or Scan the QR Code:

Nipsey Hussle Introduction

If there is one quote to describe Nipsey's entrepreneurship, it would be his own: "Be a symbol and really spark a movement." His rise from growing up in one of the worst sections of Los Angeles to become a world-renowned philanthropist is a testimony to his entrepreneurship. In this book, we are going to take an in-depth look at Nipsey Hussle in all areas of his professional life.

Nipsey Hussle's real name was Ermias Joseph Asghedom. He was known during his short lifetime mainly as a rapper. He had quite a successful run in this line of work, but he was also very big on entrepreneurship. Nipsey believed in the empowerment of black people, and he set up various businesses before his sudden and tragic demise in March of 2019.

Hussle grew up in the poverty-stricken gang environment in the heart of South Los Angeles. As he grew up, he spent most of his time hanging in the gang-infested streets and joined the Rollin 60s Crips at a young age to survive the drugs, violence and police brutality that was common with the Crenshaw District Lifestyle. Much of his lyrics describe the daily struggles of surviving the gang-mentality of the neighborhood and his way of overcoming the life he had before music.

Nipsey caught the entrepreneurial bug pretty early in life. His entrepreneurial journey began at the age of 11 when he came up with a plan to make some extra cash for himself. He began to shine shoes for $2.50 a pair. He set a goal for himself to shine about 100 shoes a day and worked hard towards it. The money he made from shining shoes went into buying school clothes and other supplies for himself. He also made some extra money selling mix tapes out of the trunk of his car.

Hussle attended Hamilton High school, considered to be a part of the pre-school to Prison pipeline, where black students experience obstacles that set them up for failure. He dropped out at fourteen after he was accused of breaking into the school's computer lab.   From then on, his life with the Rollin 60s Crips prompted a streak of petty crimes. He survived and eventually escaped the pipeline by focussing on a passion that him out of jail. His passion was music. All of these factors are reflected in his lyrics that contributed to the start of his entrepreneurial interests.

Following this quick stint with the shoe-shining business and being forced to drop out of high school, Hussle was still in his teens when he started concentrating on his music head-on. The stage name, Nipsey Hussle, was a play on the name Nipsey Russell, an iconic comedian known for breaking the stereotype barrier that defined black comics in the 60s, and it caught on. This nickname was given to Asghedom by a childhood friend, but it's worthy of note that the transition from "Russell" to "Hussle" was inspired by Hussle's unmistakable spirit of entrepreneurship.

Hussle was only twenty when he released his first independent mix tape, *Slauson Boy Volume 1*, to moderate local success. And so, his journey to success began. His mix tape helped him build quite a sizeable fan base on the west coast and put him on the right path to being signed by Cinematic Records and Epic Records. His next mix tape was released to a much larger audience and cemented his spot in the rap game. While under the label, he released two mix tapes under the *'Bullets Ain't Got No Name'* series. He collaborated with Drake on the song "Killer" and was also featured on the song "Upside Down" along with Snoop Dogg and Problem on Snoop's 09 album titled 'Malice n Wonderland'. Under the record label, Nipsey released two projects; *'Bullets Ain't Got No Name'*, as well as his first commercial single, "Hussle in the House". The record label really helped to put Nipsey Hussle's name on the map.

After the record label encountered financial problems in 2010, Hussle opted to not renew his record deal and went independent. After choosing to go independent, Hussle was chosen as one of the artistes to appear on the humanitarian song titled "We Are the World 25 for Haiti" and was featured as one of the top ten in *XXL Magazine's* "Annual Freshman Class". Nipsey was named by XXL as the "Most Determined" of his class, while *LA Weekly* called him the "next big Los Angeles MC".

According to Pat Fraser (PATMAN), Hussle's decision to go independent was in line with his belief that black people need to know more about ownership, a fact he discovered early in his career. In his interview with Julian Mitchell for Forbes, Nipsey explained how necessary it is to own your brand. Allowing your influence to add value to someone else's business (or app) that you have no ownership is giving the business free advertisement to promote your talent. For instance, if you mention your forthcoming album on a Facebook page, then thousands of your fans will buy your music. The record label gets the payoff, and you get nothing but a bit of fame.

He cautioned that all black entrepreneurs must take this into

consideration while striving to become successful.

An entrepreneur is defined as a person who starts his own

business and is willing to risk a loss in order to make money. A

hustler is defined as an aggressively enterprising person. This

combined mentality is what helped him set up his own record label,

'All Money In' in 2010. He took complete charge and ownership of

his career and released his first *All Money In Records* mix tape,

titled *The Marathon* featured guest appearances

from Kokane and MGMT, and he followed the release of Marathon

with a sequel mix tape titled *The Marathon Continues* on November

1, 2011, which featured his pal and Los Angeles rapper YG and and

Dom Kennedy from Los Angeles. He also released an album titled

Raw with rapper Blanco on April 17, 2012, with guest appearances

from a line-up of rappers like YG, Mistah FAB, B-Legit, Kokane, and a few others. The lack of creative freedom is one of the many reasons

he decided not to sign to a major record label.

Nipsey announced on September 16, 2013, that he would be

releasing a new mix tape, *Crenshaw* (hosted by DJ Drama), on

October 8, 2013. On September 24, 2013, he revealed the track list

for *Crenshaw*. It contained guest appearances from reputable artists

like Rick Ross, Slim Thug, Skeme, Sade, and a host of others.

He released another trailer for the mix tape on October 3,

2013. He was betting that if his fans valued his music, they would be

willing to pay any price for it.   In the trailer, he revealed that 1,000

hard copies of the mix tape would be sold for $100 each. This

garnered a lot of attention from fans and fellow artistes including Jay

Z, who was especially impressed by his brave marketing strategy, and

he personally bought 100 copies of the mix tape. Hussle reportedly

sold all 1,000 copies within 24 hours, effectively making $100,000.

Hussle believed in placing value on skill. This ingenious marketing strategy helped him make enough money to invest in a clothing line and technology and amassing a small fortune. The rapper was able to parlay his music career into several entrepreneurship endeavors. Nipsey Hussle's business savvy and entrepreneurial drive has been compared to several rap legends like Jay Z and Master P, who transitioned from hip hop to entrepreneurship in a similar fashion.

Nipsey Hussle was the epitome of modern time black entrepreneurship. He refused to take handouts and insisted on putting in the work it required to be a self-made man in our times. He was very good at it and became an inspiration and a beacon of hope to very many people around him. His community felt his impact all through his lifetime and was thrown into mourning when he was killed.

The rapper combined his talent and business savvy and the wisdom he learned along the way and turned himself into a successful self-made businessman. He was able to transform from a gang destined for a life of crime because he had a vision for himself and his community. He overcame many challenges by keeping his eye on the prize. "Be a symbol, spark a moment." He encouraged black businesses to follow his example to work smarter and take their brands to the next level towards making it a reality.

Nipsey Hussle's Business Ventures

1. His Record Label, ALL MONEY IN

"No need to hate me. I'm supposed to be fly/ You supposed to see my name up in lights/All money in, no money out/that' my life/ I'm walkin' out the bank, and I just made a deposit/ It's the second this week, both for a hundred thousand dollars." - Nipsey Hussle, All Money In.

Nipsey Hussle set up his own record label in 2010 after the record label he was previously signed to, Epic Records, encountered serious financial problems. He decided against signing a new deal when they got back on their feet and used the monies, he had made so far to create his own label known as *All Money In.*

It was a great opportunity for him to take control of his creative work, and he didn't mess it up. He created an opportunity for himself that so many artists today desperately seek but don't have the courage to pursue. He was able to achieve a significant amount of success without depending too much on bigger record labels.

He released his first major project, *The Marathon*, under the new label on December 21, 2010. He released other projects under his label, which included works like *The Marathon Continues* (2011), *Crenshaw* (2013), and *Mailbox Money* (2014). He also signed other artists to his label, including a group of upcoming acts from the L.A district.

The name of Nipsey's label, "All Money in, No Money Out", portrays a concept of economic self-sufficiency. Instead of spending money on things that gain no value, in save and invest in money that will create a bigger pay off in the long run.

2. Nipsey's Clothing Brand, The Marathon Store

"We was in the Regal, it was me and Steven / We done took a dream and turned it to a zenith / Anything I want and everything I needed / Gotta pace yourself, it's all about yo' breathin'/ You can have it all, it's all about your reason / I done took my name and carved it in the cement." - Nipsy Hussle, Blue Laces 2, Victory Lap

This is us trying to fuse hip-hop, fashion and tech… I think we're in the process of seeing technology integrated with everything, become a part of the world. — Nipsey Hussle

While talking to Billboard, Nipsey described his business model of a brick and mortar store that integrates technology with retail.

The model to execute this idea would be the Apple Store. Smart store uses techniques and technology to offer a more personal shopping experience. A customer can receive messages about a product, price and any discounts. The customer can use an app to preview exclusive content, see instantly if the product is in stock, and the purchase can be paid through the phone. The merchandise sold is exclusive to The Marathon Clothing store ranging from t-shirts, sweat suits, hats, lighters, masks and music products.

Hussle opened the clothing store on June 17, 2017 along with partners Steve Carless, Karen Civil, and his brother, Samiel Asghedom. Hussle insisted on opening the store at an intersection in the Crenshaw commercial district. This was important to him because he wanted to be able to invest and provide jobs and opportunities in his neighborhood of Hyde Park.

The location had always held a special place in the "Double Up" rapper's heart. Hussle used to sell his mix tapes in the parking lot of the strip mall long before he opened the shop. He eventually

started to rent a place there and bought it when the landlord tried to

evict him. Hussle explained that he was hustling in this parking lot

long before he was renting. It's just always been a hub for local

entrepreneurs.

In May 2019, the store shared a message to its customers via

its Instagram page, announcing the discontinuation of physical

operations due to the overwhelming demand following the Hussle's

untimely demise. However, the store noted that its online store was

going to be operational around the clock in order to serve customers.

Also, plans had been set in place to make the building into a

multipurpose center, which would be named "The Nipsey Hussle

Tower." According to The Los Angeles Times, the establishment

would include a museum, residential living area with affordable

rates, retail and dining shops that will offer jobs. The details are

limited, and plans have been on hold.

However, since his passing, the store has become a tribute center of sorts for fans and lovers of the Crenshaw rapper. It became a sacred focal point where fans, family, and friends go to mourn the late rapper.

The profits from the store now go to the family that Nipsey Hussle left behind. He is survived by two kids: Kross Asghedom and Emani. Hussle had his son, Kross, with Lauren London (actress and former girlfriend of Lil Wayne), whom he dated from 2013 up until his recent demise. He had Emani during the early stages of his career while he was dating Emani's mother, Tanisha Foster.

The "Dedication" rapper is also survived by his parents, brother, and sister.

3. The STEM Hub He Co-Founded, Too Big to Fail/Vector90

"As an entrepreneur, as an investor, I'm trying to be as educated as I can to where the progression of technology capability is going and what it does to these different categories that, me as an artist and an influencer, I can get involved and bring value." - Nipsey Hussle

Nipsey Hussle is replacing the pre-school to prison pipeline with his own inner-city to Silicon Valley bridge called Vector90. The goal is to promote creativity and networking that connects inner-city centers to the global center for innovation and high-technology. The inaugural center is located in Los Angeles. It is considered a coworking space with private offices, shared workspaces, and business/commercial grade IT support. According to its website, the center also offers professional and social events and a wide range of amenities from beverages to front desk service to encourage social interaction. Vector90 houses a STEM program/center for inner-city youth called "Too Big to Fail". The plan is to extend the program with other inner cities across the US in an effort to increase diversity in STEM. The name comes from an economic theory that the collapse of certain businesses (such as Facebook or Bank of America) would be catastrophic to the community.

Nipsey Hussle, along with one of his business partners David Gross, jointly founded this science, technology, engineering and math (STEM) hub in 2018. Its inaugural program brought STEM companies to the Crenshaw community, a move that was considered unthinkable without Nipsey's support. Hussle shared with the LA Times that as a kid growing up, he was always looking for somebody that cared rather than accepting handouts. The young version of himself sought people who were passionate about creating impactful change and thought beyond their own self-interests. And this was one of the inspirations behind his resolve to create opportunities for kids who had interests in science and technology. He wanted to give them, at the very least, a fighting chance.

Hussle was popular for his dedication to his childhood district of Crenshaw. He was one of the few successful people from the district who invested in the community and made sure that the proceeds from his various ventures were leveraged to build and uplift the community. He was passionate about creating resources to empower the kids growing up in the Crenshaw community.

4. The Marathon Agency

"The marathon agency is the new home for the RADICALS...The REVOLUTIONARIES AND THE GAME CHANGERS that believe they can do it their way." - Nipsy Hussle

The trio of Steve Carless, Karen Civil, and Jorge Peniche, blended their combined skills in business and marketing with an original idea known as "The Marathon Agency." Founded in 2013, the agency came together to help their clientele shape and execute disruptive campaigns and concepts. Hussle was heavily and directly

involved with the goings-on at the Marathon Agency. He was the

silent partner that invested a vision and the funding for this agency

that attracts a diverse set of talented people in all stages of their

individual careers. The agency has been responsible for several

ingenious marketing and media strategies for several big names such

as Nicki Minaj, Jeezy, Nick Cannon, and a host of other popular acts

in the music industry.

In a piece about Hussle's popular #Proud2pay campaign, the

Billboard Magazine praised the Marathon Agency for executing a

grand campaign like Hussle's $100 Crenshaw mix tape campaign

which had already been released free streaming online, but the

agency created a campaign and structure that allowed his fans to

directly support him.

Given the success of their first official collaboration as artist

and agency, the partners in the agency joined forces again for

Nipsey's *Mailbox Money* mix tape in 2014, upping the ante with a similar model, but this time charging $1,000 for 100 physical copies that also came with a ticket to an advanced listening of his highly anticipated album *Victory Lap*. It was with the help of the Marathon Agency that Nick Cannon became Chief Creative Officer for RadioShack. The name was coined a marathon — "a journey...a race at your own pace racing against yourself," — from Hussle's Marathon branding that inspired its mission statement.

Carless also stated that they continually sought out Nipsey on issues that had to do with the agency because of his non-unilateral world view and laser-sharp focus on things. He praised Nipsey as someone who wasn't whimsical when it comes to giving insights on creative stuff and always went his gut.

5. His Interests and Investments in Real Estate

"I got a PJ for the whole crew/passport looking old news/champagne in a glasshouse/old money knows what I'm about/put your money in that real estate." *- Nipsey Hussle, Real Estate, Royalty*

Nipsey Hussle owned all of the property on which his various businesses were built and he was particular about it being in the environment that he grew up in. Hussle opened the flagship store of his clothing brand, The Marathon Clothing, in a strip mall where he used to hang out in Crenshaw and where he sold his mix tapes out of a trunk in the parking lot. He and his business partner, David Gross, eventually bought up the whole property and had big plans for a restaurant and barbershop amongst other businesses.

Unfortunately, Nipsey was killed outside of his store in the plaza, and it now serves as a place for thousands of mourners to pay their respects and celebrate his life.

The plans for the plaza have been put on hold indefinitely.

Business Lessons Learned from Nipsey Hussle

1. Ownership is Very Important:

"I just believe in ownership...I believe in investing in yourself...your foundation should be strong." - Nipsey Hussle

Hussle, aside from the entrepreneurial spirit which he already had, was heavily influenced by the lives of music moguls like Jay Z, Diddy and others who have ownership of all their content and work. He was very aware of industry rule #4080 (record company people are shady, a rule reminding artiste not to trust anybody whose actions in a particular situation are driven by the urge to make money), and he promised to never go down that path if he could help it.

His record label, All Money In, was created in 2010 after many terrible record deals. He promised himself to do better by the artistes that were signed under him, and he did. In an interview with The Fader, he told them that, while coming up, he learned the rules of playing with money and brought that mentality into music. Nipsey invested heavily in most of his business ventures, especially in his music career. Hussle personally funded most of his career by buying music equipment and other studio amenities at a young age when he could have easily spent his money on cars and jewelry as his peers would have, but Nipsey was all about putting money into what you believe in, hence the personal investment in his career.

Nipsey also worked towards buying (and eventually bought) up the property that housed his clothing business, The Marathon Store, and had plans to expand and open up more businesses, including a restaurant and barbershop at the same strip mall.

2. Know Your Value*:*

"I believe that economics is based on scarcity of markets and it's possible to monetize your art without compromising the integrity for commerce." - Nipsey Hussle

In 2013, The Crenshaw mix tape was released as free to stream online. Nipsey also released 1,000 hard copies of a limited numbered of signed first edition for $100 each, and he included a ticket to an upcoming show. It seemed ridiculous at the time, and nobody thought anybody would pay such a steep price for a mix tape, but the world was proven wrong. He sold all 1,000 copies, with Jay Z personally purchasing 100 copies, and grossed $100,000 in 24 hours.

"Fans will pay you your worth, so put a price on it - $1000 Album." - Nipsey Hussle

He released his next project with a $1,000 price tag on each unit and sold 60 units. It proved to the world that he had a loyal, dedicated fan base that knew his value. It also showed the world that, when people believe in your art, they'll happily pay whatever price tag you put on it. He encouraged pricing your product on what you believe it's worth and don't settle for what you *think* they'll pay.

We never see the benefits until we realize the value. Everyone has the potential, and Nipsey Hussle realized this very early on in life. Using that logic, he attached great value to himself and defined and controlled his own destiny. He took his great potential, harnessed it and recorded resounding success from it. He took what he had and made it work for him. This is what all black entrepreneurs should strive to achieve.

Nipsey, while speaking to Forbes contributor Julian Mitchell, wanted to explain why he chose to go independent and wanted to prove to people undervaluing their influence as independent artists.

In his explanation, Nipsey said, when people clamor for followership on Twitter and they get their target number (in his example, he said 10 million people), he believes that the individual has simply used their influence to add value to the social media network which they had no stake or ownership in.

Nipsey using Twitter as an example for an interview with inc.com. If he estimated the worth of each user to be around $21 and, when the company submits its valuation at the end of the day and gets a big paycheck as a result of selling the company, the individual who helped to draw followership on the platform doesn't get a share despite the fact that they helped to boost the valuation of the company.

He said most people who understand the business of valuation and Silicon Valley ecosystem company just choose to forget this simple yet important fact about the power of a large user base. Nipsey also made an example of what he and his co-founders did with Cuddlr and explained that the big takeaway from the company which they eventually sold was in the strength of the hundreds and thousands of users they had to make it valuable enough to exit and cash out. He also made mention of Facebook and Atlantic Records and explained that what made them successful was their billion users and the strong artists involved.

Still, as Hussle wisely said, we keep fighting to get more followers, and we worry about vanity metrics on these platforms. At the end of the day, when these companies go public and record profits, we get nothing out of it. We have basically worked for these companies for free..

During the interview with VladTv, Nipsey explained why he wouldn't sign with a major record label because the structure put in place by this recording label does not enable them to respect the talent of artistes.

He said the manner of engagement some of the recording labels employ when talking to upcoming artistes is so disrespectful because they don't deem the artiste worthy of any negotiation talks until he becomes successful. Rather they prefer to talk to a third party affiliated with the artiste rather than the artiste himself.

He would rather they respect him as an artiste first before signing any record deal. In his words, he said he would rather the recording label sees him as the executive representing the talent, not just the talent.

Using this approach, he believes that the conversation with the recording label will be much different than the typical conversation they've had with upcoming artistes.

3. Understand and Directly Connect with Your Audience

"I realized the power of hip-hop. I realized how influential this music and this culture are." - Nipsey Hussle

"A lot of artists come into the game with a radio record, but they don't establish the fans as fans of their style of music. It's just that they're a fan of that song, and after that song plays out, it's real hard for 'em". - Nipsey Hussle

Nipsey Hussle was everything from talented, hardworking, smart, and ambitious, amongst other things, but his real secret was a connection. He was able to, time and time again, create unique, exclusive experiences for his fan base and community. The entire premise of his clothing brand, The Marathon Store, was for people to be able to come in and have an all-round immersive experience. He was all about building interactive spaces for the consumer and, as stated above, skipping traditional social media shortcuts for genuine

communication.

His notoriety and popularity majorly came from connecting

with his audience (and not the other way around). Nipsey wasn't

waiting on a co-sign to build a movement -- and he was able to

inspire more non-traditional entrepreneurs in his short life because

of it.

During an interview, he was asked why he had such laser-

focus on his fans.

He explained that his experience as a rap fan influenced his

fan-based approach to his music. According to him, he believed some

artiste, after amassing a fan base with their content, tend to deviate

from the content that attracted the fans to them initially because of commercial gains but eventually, he believes they always make a

turnaround to the content they were initially known for.

Nipsey believed his approach as an artiste in the game

wouldn't base off of commercial gains but rather with the content he

is known and represents in order to produce something authentic

and genuine for his fans.

In the interview which was recorded in his Crenshaw hood,

he further elaborated on how global the world has become through

the internet and how it gave him as an upcoming artiste the

opportunity to reach a global audience, and he believed he could

leverage that global following to alter the dynamics of the typical

agreement record labels offer "hot" upcoming artistes. In his words,

"my main focus was to leverage the global underground to create an

unprecedented type of situation."

Also, in another interview, he mentioned how he transitioned from making music for money to get a record deal with a major label to understanding that, in the real scheme of things, his music shouldn't be made for the label as they were just middlemen.

Nipsey Hussle reasoned that if music was created solely with the people or fans in mind, then that's the best strategy as he believed that making music to please your label or platform wasn't the best way to create a quality body of music.

Because of this deep connection he shared with people, there were calls for a petition to have the Slauson Avenue and Crenshaw Boulevard intersection near Hussle's store Marathon Clothing renamed as "Nipsey Hussle Square". On the day of his funeral, the council reiterated the plan to rename the intersection Ermias "Nipsey Hussle" Asghedom Square to honor him and his contributions to the neighborhood.

His death drew a lot of artistic responses as over 50 murals dedicated to the rapper were seen in different areas in the City of Los Angeles. One mural is in an alley near the strip mall where he was killed.

4. Be Prepared to Put in the Work:

"When you let go of your pride, you'll find a lesson in your pain." - Nipsey Hussle, Bulgari Shades, TMC X-Tra Laps

Nipsey Hussle knew no one was going to give him any handouts. He knew he had to put in the work himself, and he did it. He woke up every day, determined to grind and grind until he achieved his goals.

Being self-made also means taking challenges and never making excuses for non-performance and failure. Hussle could have used his tumultuous gang past as an excuse to not make something of himself, but he did not. He did the opposite. He left no room for laziness, and he cultivated good habits.

He was completely dedicated to his music and quickly mastered and got used to the grind and hard work that came with it. He built a strong small team, and never stopped to look back on past failures. This is something every black entrepreneur and independent artist should emulate.

Success did not stop him from being ready to get down and get dirty to do tasks that other artists of his caliber might have considered to be below them.

Nipsey Hussle's success could be attributed to his humility and his hands-on approach no matter how menial the work was, from building his basement studio to taking out the trash, no task was below him. For instance, at a very young age, he had such an entrepreneurial mindset that he decided to "shine shoes" to make money. And along the path to his success, Nipsey stayed willing to learn and participate in every aspect in every stage by doing the most basic things.

"Most people want to skip the process, not knowing that when you skip, steps you miss lessons." - Nipsey Hussle

Nipsey was known for saying that he couldn't give any person power over his process, nor could a person make or break him except if he does so himself or God does.

5. Don't Give Up

*"Everybody get their game tested. If you don't quit, you gon'
learn. And you gon' figure things out. That's really the secret to
everything is how much you can take. How much pressure, how much
stress, how much insecurity in your decisions, all of that... Stay down,
it's a marathon." - Nipsey Hussle*

After more than a decade of work and a boatload of mix
tapes, Nipsy Hussle finally got his first Grammy nomination in 2019.
He hustled and worked hard for over a decade nonstop without
giving up. While many of his peers would have given up along the
way in pursuit of other careers, he didn't. He knew what he wanted,
and he did not stop working for it until his very untimely death.
Nipsey was a personality who had bigger and broader goals that had
the potential of pushing his legacy long into the future.

Hussle narrated how he gave up on the rap music for seven months, but he always found himself coming back and decided he wasn't quitting anymore.

"You've got to have faith in what you're doing and not take no for an answer." - Nipsey Hussle

6. You Will Always Reap the Seed You Sow

"Still, somehow I understood that I could make the seed grow, and that one day that tree will bear fruit to feed my people." - Nipsey Hussle

Going on about reaping his hard work, he remembered a time he was doing only music and was committed to it at age 19 but was suffering financially as opposed to the high-flyer lifestyle he was used to.

Then the police raided his studio and took all his equipment, took his shotgun, which was registered, but he was on probation and shouldn't be around guns.

So, when this incident happened, he was confused as he had chosen to commit himself to the music and leave the gang life.

Due to this incident, Nipsey had to leave music for a while again in order to make ends meet but went back to it when a partner from Epic records reached out to sign him despite the fact that he had not done any promotion or released any new work plus he had financial troubles.

This was when he realized all that trouble that went before and during the raid eventually paid off.

"Be truthful with yourself and other people, and try your best to make decisions outside of your ego." - Nipsey Hussle.

7. Have a Plan

"If you have a plan, it's not just like a pipe dream. You have a step-by-step list of things to do to get to your goal." - Nipsey Hussle

Nipsey can be described as a meticulous man. He believed in doing things systematically in order to achieve goals, and it's this mindset that formed some of his popular moves like the decision to stay independent.

In an interview about why he didn't take cheques from the big recording companies, he said he needed to be in a place where the companies don't just offer him any deal they deem fit, but rather, he would determine the details of the deal.

So in an interview about having a plan, the late Nipsey advised that one of the most important things to do in order to be successful is to get rid of all your doubts, as doubts would only serve as hindrances to your goal. According to him, to get rid of all doubts, you needed to make a plan because, without a plan, all you have is just a pipe dream.

According to Nipsey Hussle, it was important you had a step-by-step list of things to do to get to your goal because failure to do this will really make it very hard to really have faith in what you're doing because in his words "as soon as somethings pop up, it's going to look like the end," but if you had a game plan of everything you needed to do when one thing pops up, then you're not caught unawares and can go ahead to achieve your goal despite the

obstacles you encounter at each of the steps you set.

*"Without a game plan and without a strong sense of faith in
what you're doing, it's going to be really hard to accomplish
anything."* - Nipsey Hussle

8. Be Proud of What You're Doing

*"I'm at peace with what I'm doing, I feel good with what I
wake up doing and about my lifestyle. At one point, I wasn't proud of
my lifestyle...Now I wake up with the feeling that I'm going in the
direction that I'm here for."* - Nipsey Hussle

As an entrepreneur, you need to understand what you're getting into and be willing to show it off proudly. This is one of the lessons that can be derived from the late Nipsey Hussle.

While speaking on the importance of being proud of what you do, Hussle narrated that during the early stages of his life, he had a street hustler/gang-banger lifestyle and on the surface, although he seemed happy about it, he wasn't content.

However, since he discovered music and stayed committed to it, he narrated that he goes about his day with a feeling of self-content as he believes what he is doing and seeking to attain is much bigger than the kind of lifestyle he once he lived.

"What am I on this planet for, I'm doing it. Bigger than just the L.A., bigger than some gang-banging, bigger than some street

shit. Just on some human shit, I'm doing what I'm here to do." -

Nipsey Hussle

The lesson here is once you find something that you're passionate about, you're bound to feel good about yourself, and a feeling of self-contentment overwhelms you and everything else.

9. Don't Listen to Detractors

"It's strictly bizness in this game/still they faking friendly/Don't let them take advantage of you in and make them envy." - Nipsey Hussle, Play Top Floor, TMC X-Tra Laps

"It can be as simple as it seems, if you never doubt yourself and learn from everything you see, no wishing on a star can turn your life in a dream." - Nipsey Hussle

During the course of your entrepreneurial journey, you are bound to meet a lot of obstacles that would distract you from achieving the results you seek to achieve, and the late Nipsey Hussle gives advice on how to never listen to the "little man."

According to him, with his respect to pushing himself to attain his musical fame, Nipsey said he approached his musical career in a deliberate and determined way as he immersed himself entirely into the process —from making the music, mastering, recording, promotion, meetings with labels and signing of any form deal. In his words,

"I put my first foot forward to the street with my mix tape series. This was all me..." - Nipsey Hussle

He never for once had the "impossibility notion," and this is what he said drove him. When a member of his team told him something couldn't be done, he would go ahead to do that thing not just on a whim but because he has studied and understood the game before making the decision.

10. Keep Evolving

"I think everybody's trying to get to a place in themselves where they conquer what they was afraid of; they achieved some of their life goals, keep their word about what they were trying to do.

As an entrepreneur, you need to constantly self-develop yourself as this is a major indicator of success and progress, and a big part of evolving is learning.

"I'm focusing on my music, but I still got a cold library of books that I've either read or I plan on getting to." - Nipsey Hussle

On the issue of evolving, Nipsey uses the example of his rap career and how he had to constantly improve to make sure his next project was always better than the last. On an Instagram, Nipsey encourage reading books to become aware of many different ways of thinking.

Nipsey co-authored a book reflecting his journey. The Marathon Continues: A hood tale of Nipsey Hussle (co-author with Eugene L. Weems) was published posthumously in April 2019, to promote literacy in urban communities

He credits Uell Andersen for enlightening him about releasing the powers that one already possesses within them in "Three Magic Words."

In his song title *Blue Laces 2*, he makes mention to "The Spook by the Door" by Sam Greenlee. This fiction tells the tale of a former gang member in Chicago turned CIA officer who uses the CIA tactics to stand up against the American government.

He acknowledges the idea for charging $100 for his mixtape came from "Contagious: Why Things Catch On," by Jonah Berger. This is the true story of a restaurant owner in Philadephia, who successfully sold and created a demand for a $100 cheesesteak.

He praises "Power vs Force" by David R. Hawkins. This book suggested he rethink dealing with disagreements by asking the question: "Are you arguing to be right, or are you trying to reveal the truth."

"Even as you make progress, you need the discipline to keep from backtracking and sabotaging the success as it's happening." - Nipsey Hussle

11. Loyalty

"I done made so many millions/Ain't nothin' to think about, because I am the one that still come back even though I made it out...and loyalty, I swear that's everything." - Nipsey Hussle, Bigger than Life.

This is probably one of the most important aspects of being an entrepreneur. The need to have a family-like team is a fundamental aspect of your success, and Nipsey had his opinion on how important loyalty is.

Using his rap career as a reference, he mentioned how their culture on loyalty on his team is clearly obvious at his shows and concerts, as people can see that his team is enjoying what they do and seeing it as fun rather than as a normal day-time job.

In his words, you will know loyalty when you see it.

"It's organic, and the industry bull usually doesn't get in the way of success when it's like that when it's family-oriented. It don't cause the natural fall-outs that happen with people when you be successful." - Nipsey Hussle

12. Make Sacrifices

"Dedication, hard work plus patience/the sum of all my sacrifice/I'm done waiting'/told you I wasn't playin'/Now your what I've been saying...its dedication." - Nipsey Hussle, Dedication, Victory Lap

Being an entrepreneur means making certain sacrifices to get to your goal, and a perfect example is the sacrifice approach Nipsey Hussle used to attain the success he achieved with his rap career.

Nipsey advised that in life sometimes you needed to take ten steps back to take two forward, and using his life as an example, he said at one point on his musical journey, he had to let go of some of his luxuries like jewelry, everyday money, cars, etc. and go back to being a young dude that was pinching every penny in order to stay creative and work.

In his words about the impact of the resolution, *"It was hard for my ego."*

13. Live Your Dream

"Living in a dream/where everybody loves me/I'm living in a dream world/How'd I get so lucky?" - Nipsey Hussle, Livin' in a Dream, Hard to Imagine the Neighborhood Ever Changing.

There is no doubt that Nipsey Hussle lived his dream as both an entrepreneur and a rap star.

According to him, success was simply being able to do what you got to do and support yourself off of it, and he believed he was successful because he was doing what he loved (music) and wasn't living his old life any longer.

And also, he pointed out success involves maintaining and being content with the lifestyle of being able to do what he loved daily.

14. Diversifying

"The value is created in content, so when I think of us as hip-hop artists…the primary responsibility is one and the same. To create content, but we don't have a product line." - Nipsey Hussle

Apart from being a rapper, Nipsey Hussle was a serial entrepreneur. Content marketing is marketing a brand. In Nipsey's case, it was his Marathon Clothing store where exclusive items are sold. Another coined idea is Mailbox money, which is passive income – putting your time and money that will reward you in your mailbox every month. Some traditional examples are real estate and the stock market, building an online empire is setting up a website where your licensed items are sold, and lending your time and money to a

business in which you will get a return. Nipsey funneled his time and

money into his Marathon Agency.

He believed that everything doesn't go in one direction; there

will be ups and downs on your journey. So, if you have a surplus and

you're doing well in an area, it pays to diversify to other business

ventures just in case the main business fails, so you have something

to fall back on.

Also, he was of the opinion that by diversifying, he was able

to make pure music and not make music for money as he had other

streams of income.

Nipsey Hussle on Keys of Building Wealth

"Instead of trying to build a brick wall, lay a brick every day. Eventually, you'll look up, and you'll have a brick wall." - Nipsey Hussle,

Nipsey's formula for building wealthy centers around ownership. To own something is very important, and to understand investments and to live within your means and also make something was one of the most critical things for him. According to Nipsey, some have mastered the rap game but consume so fast that they can't get ahead.

His father took him and his younger brother on a three-month trip to his father's homeland, Eritrea, East Africa. He saw a community whose love and peace went beyond the desire for money. This was a cause he could bring back to the Crenshaw district through a concept known a community activism or as investing in an ecosystem. His community grew along with his success.

An ecosystem is a community of living things sharing an environment. Nipsey contributed to his ecosystem - Crenshaw and Hyde Park communities. He revitalized playgrounds and paved basketball courts.

With Vector90, he rented space and offer seed money to start-up entrepreneurs within the Crenshaw district.

Nipsey co-branded with Puma to endorse products for his company - Marathon Clothing. His iconic brand was the core of his line of footwear and clothing.

Nipsey has partnered with a local Fatburger and opened a dispensary that sells the only true strain of Marathon OG. He has also invested in Vezt Inc.

"Start with what you know and grow." - Nipsey Hussle.

Nipsey knew music. With his unique marketing strategy selling his Crenshaw mix tape, he could continue to release his music digitally and sell limited first editions tapes for $100 each. This gave him the seed money to fund his All Money In label.

Nipsey knew what was needed to revitalize his neighborhood. Under the Opportunity Zone legislation, tax cuts are given to encourage long-term investing in economically-distressed communities. Nipsey developed plans to offer affordable housing and food and jobs via his Hyde Park real estate project.

Nipsey Hussle On Cryptocurrency

"Any time a country transitions to a fiat currency [paper money], they collapse. That's just world history; you don't have to know about cryptocurrency to know that." - Nipsey Hussle

To better understand cryptocurrency, you need to understand the concept behind eCommerce. Simply stated, eCommerce is a commercial transaction that happens over the internet. An example of e-commerce is Amazon, which is a third-party eCommerce seller.

Nipsey believed strongly in this concept of buying and selling on the internet and transferring money electronically. The exchange of funds doesn't have to a physical form like paper (fiat) money because each transaction forms a blockchain.

A blockchain is a digital diary of transactions. For every transaction, you need an address and a string of numbers that identify the transaction. An easily recognizable example is PayPal.

Fiat money is a currency that is not backed up with precious metals (gold and silver). An example is the US dollar bill. At one point, each bill labelled silver certificate was backed up with a specific amount of silver coins. Now they are considered "banknotes" with each note (dollar bill) has no value other than what the government places on it.

One of the opportunities he invested in was a cryptocurrency company called Follow Coin. The company is based on following and replicating the trading decision of top and successful traders of crypto in real-time.

Nipsey's reason for investing at the time was because the penetration was smaller but had the potential of getting increased penetration with time, and it was best to invest in it early before it blows. Market penetration is a measure of how much a product is being used by customers.   For instance, Coca-Cola is an example. It's a product that's been around for over a century and is marketed everywhere in the world. Coca-Cola has developed other products beyond its original flavor (for instance, Diet Coke or Sprite) and sells them to existing markets all over the world to increase sales for the company. Coca-Cola has penetrated the markets, meaning it's easily recognized by customers in the beverage market.

The Move Behind the $100 Mix-Tape

It was one of the genius marketing tactics Nipsey was known for.

When asked how he pulled it off, he said he read a book called *Contagious* by Jonah Berger which revolved around a $100 cheesesteak in Philadelphia, and he believed that gave him inspiration combined with the knowledge that each artiste had a fraction of fan base; some fans were highly engaged and while some were mildly committed, and, as such, whatever price you call was the amount they committed fans were willing to pay.

The price tag to him was sort of a way for the listener to reciprocate what the music did for them with a tag line that says "Always by choice never by force" because the music was already on other free and paid platforms, so it was the user's choice to pick

what they wanted.

In short, it proved he could use his street-smart hustle to

prove to the world he could be a legitimate businessman and a

consummate artist.

Time-Management and Work-Personal Life Balance

"On a mission, your worst enemy is idle time." - Nipsey Hussle

In an interview with Source magazine, Nipsey shared some helpful tips for entrepreneurs, and one of the tips he discussed was how to manage your time.

According to him, time management and discipline is about identifying where you get the most effective return on energy. In his opinion, you need to figure this out and concentrate your energy there.

Nipsey said for someone like him who has dabbled into various businesses, the most effective return on energy for him was when he was in his studio making music.

"When I'm in that booth, I can do something in that moment that changes my life forever at any moment." - Nipsey Hussle

He believed that although he was capable of being as good in his other business, the "impact of return on the energy" from his music was unrivaled compared to his other ventures.

Also, in the same interview, he gave an insight on how to balance personal life with work.

He mentioned how a statement by Birdman inspired his approach to make the workplace, sociable and comfortable and an entertaining place, and this was hinged on the notion that if he had to leave the studio to do personal things, then the time to do those personal things will cut into productivity at the workplace and in his words, "we're not really going to be able to get an edge over ourself and definitely not over the competition."

Still, on the issue of balancing work life with personal life, he said the issue of time management involves sacrificing, and he mentioned that during his teenage years, he wasn't a very social person, and he would wonder at times if he was wasting those moments of youth when he could have had fun instead of working.

However, over the years he realized that act of sacrificing your fun times as a teen was the distinguishing factor and this sacrifice he posits doesn't end with the teenage years, but rather as you grow, you need to figure what else you could give up to have an advantage over your former self and figuring this out would help you in mastering your 24 hours.

Also, in the interview, he gave a description of a typical day in his life.

First, he mentioned that he handles his core responsibilities first early in the morning then work. Then, have a cut-off time where he can satisfactorily say to himself that he had done all the work for that and take another activity that wasn't necessarily work-related, which he said could be reading a book, watching a documentary or talking to somebody smart.

All these efforts he believed are geared towards making sure he is getting better every day.

Nipsey Hussle on How to Make Money

It is no secret that the Late Nipsey Hussle was a serial entrepreneur and invested in various streams of income.

So, his advice on making it would remain ever-green.

For Nipsey Hussle, for young men to be financially independent, they need to be a worker first and commit to working daily and have an entrepreneurial creative mind-set and use their resources to create something that they own or control.

On how to make money, here is the advice he said he would give his own son at the time.

So, the first and most effective thing to do on the journey to

making money, according to Nipsey Hussle, was to be a worker first

and commit to working on something daily.

The next step is to make plans that the work you do is not

leveraged by other people, and he attributes this notion to a book he

read titled *Political Economy,* a book which he said broke down the

United States wage formula and how wages are determined.

According to him, the book explained that BIG company at

the highest level of their business strategy determined how much

they were going to pay their employees based on a multiple and that

multiple is usually 10x. The company then decides that whatever the

worker's labor is worth, the worker should be paid 1/10th of that. So,

if a worker's labor is worth $100 an hour, then that worker will be

paid $10 an hour.

His reaction to this insight was that the whole wage arrangement was a trap and hence, the need for young black men to think and become entrepreneurial in their approach as the idea of having other leverage on their work or labor wasn't healthy.

He advised that young black men should seek to create and build their own enterprise regardless of the means through which they seek to achieve that. In his words, "whether it's washing cars or shining shoes, if it's yours, then you have your hands on the steering wheel."

Nipsey narrated that growing up, he knew people had too much pride to be or do certain things, but they didn't have too much pride to be broke.

So, he said he would advise his son on the integrity and pride that comes with hard work, ownership, and control. Also, he said he would advise that he choose a less glamorous position over a glamorous one as long as the former allows him to have control of the steering wheel, as there is no other option to really be financially independent.

Nipsey said to upgrade in the entrepreneurial space depends on how clever and how creative you can maneuver through obstacles and the ability to *leverage all of your resources towards creating something that you own or control.*

Nipsey Hussle's Financial Mistakes

One rule Nipsey Hussle shared to avoid financial self-sabotage is spending below your means, and he attributed this culture of making money and blowing it quickly with the black culture.

He explained that the first thing to avoid financial self-sabotage is the avoidance of the culture of living and spending above your means and this culture he said is very common within the black community which he said is not exempted from but believes that most black young men are victims of this "spending-above-your-means culture" as opposed to the owners of these enterprises young black men patronize who are worth millions but do not spend on frivolities rather they build legacies that set up their families for generations.

So, Nipsey advised that the way out for the black young man

is *to be outside of that expectation that is usually attached with a*

being a successful young black man as he believes that most of these

expectations are not in alignment with what is going to keep him

wealthy and create generational wealth.

Nipsey Hussle on Maintaining Longevity of a Brand

As an entrepreneur, longevity is important but it's very hard to maintain, but Nipsey Hussle helps out with this as he uses his music career as an example on how to maintain longevity of a brand.

He believes that the secret to building longevity in the rap industry was when the artiste viewed his career as a relationship between the artiste and his fans. If the artiste doesn't violate the principles that are the foundation of that relationship by changing what the artiste is known for with consistent show of growth and progress, then the artiste can build a fan base of loyal fans that would contribute to his longevity in the industry.

However, if the artiste chooses to mix things up by being inconsistent in his output and the image his fans perceive of him, then the artiste would have problems.

He also mentioned the importance of *being honorable and being solid in the long run as most people who had great moments but later did something that compromised their image tend to lose their influence and following because of their actions.*

"*People will respect you on how you conduct yourself, and we don't listen to people we don't respect. I know I don't. It's very hard to listen to somebody you don't respect.*" - Nipsey Hussle

"*No matter how good it may sound aesthetically in your mind, you're thinking this dude is a clown. This girl is a clown. I don't want to hear nothing coming out of her mouth.*" - Nipsey Hussle

The principle of an artiste seeing his career as a relationship, according to Nipsey Hussle, is a universal principle and an ingredient of success for the artiste.

Nipsey Hussle on Creating Brand Awareness

In a recorded video hang-out with Gary Vaynerchuk, Nipsey Hussle discussed the topic of hacking distribution and creating awareness.

"When I used to go hand to hand and grind, I used to bootleg CDs, I used to sell a lot of this shit to drugs too. My CD, I used to sell, and I used to have to distinguish myself for five seconds. So, I used to be like bro, if this is garbage, throw it out the window and that would make 'em be like, let me see this shit. You feel me? If it's trash, throw that shit out the window right in front of me, I ain't trippin'. Just listen. You feel me? And it's free. Check it out. You know, if it's boo boo, throw that shit out the window, bro." - Nipsey Hussle

Nipsey Hussle on Building an Eco-System

So far, all of the aims and goals of these moves made by Nipsey Hussle is towards creating what he describes as an ecosystem.

According to him, his plan was to create a wholesome system similar to that of Apple's model whereby production down to the point of consumption was handled exclusively by the company especially in terms of the music business, and in his opinion, there was no structure that allowed the artiste to control the supply of their work and also own their masters.

In his opinion, Jay Z was the only artiste in hip-hop who had the opportunity to have such a structure in place, and this already set him up for success as he owned his masters and had a say in distribution and everything involved in making an artiste successful.

Nipsey said his ultimate goal was to have something similar to this which he described clearly and also emphasized the importance and value of an ecosystem.

His plan was to have ten marathon stores in different parts of the globe where he could drop a thousand units in each store at $100 each, which will eventually fetch him a revenue of about a million dollars after selling 10,000 units.

Nipsey believed that by creating a system whereby all these parts are interlinked, it would allow for more freedom to create a good and quality body of work, build a brand and also develop a stronger relationship with fans.

Although Nipsey is no more, his lessons and ideology still live on…it's safe to say that Nipsey's Marathon still continues.

Nipsey Hussle's Quotes

Nipsey Hussle had a lot of wise sayings during speaking engagements and interviews. His interviews were so value-laded that the Game said, you could hear an entire album of Nipsey Hussle by just listening to Nipsey's interviews.

His quotes cover a wide range of themes: entrepreneurship, luck, failure, integrity, respect, planning, time management and these quotes relate to various people from different walks of life in different ways.

His quotes and statements are capable of inspiring and gives you an insight on the kind of mindset you should have as an entrepreneur or an artiste who seeks to be successful or wishes to follow the Nipsey Hussle's Marathon Blueprint.

On the themes of planning, luck, and failure, one consistent thing that can be deduced from his quotes on these themes is the need to have a solid plan and see luck as a reward for preparedness as well as seeing failure as a necessary evil but not giving in to it.

While on the themes of entrepreneurship, respect, and time management, he consistently advises the need to put self-respect first, to always seek to create and own your labor, to avoid being disrespected, and to consistently improve yourself to avoid losing influence.

Nipsey spread his wisdom not only through interviews but also in his music. Each time his lyrics run through a listener's mind, his words are repeated until the message is understood.

"I try to sprinkle a little gems and jewels in the music that people could use in their own life." - Nispey Hussle

Conclusion and Summary

He started from humble beginnings in the ghetto area of Crenshaw, then going ahead to do petty businesses like shining shoes to hustling on the streets selling mix tapes from the trunk of his car to making one of the most revolutionizing moves in the industry at the time by selling his Crenshaw mix tape for a $100 and selling it out in 24 hours.

The Journey of Nipsey Hussle to fame was that of a man who was deliberate in steps and understood what he wanted and went for it.

Rapper, The Game, during an interview was talking about how he first met Nipsey Hussle said he was driving through the Crenshaw neighborhood when Nipsey and a couple of his friends just pulled up to him and gave him his CD.

The Game commented on the audacity of the approach which was unlike the typical upcoming artiste move.

All these stories reiterate the fact Nipsey Hussle was a guy who was confident in his ability to excel at anything he set his mind to.

Nipsey Hussle was a man who wore many hats and managed to excel in almost all the aspects he delved into, and this does not come as a surprise as his mindset and his blueprint to approach his situation are mostly similar across all his ventures.

To some, Nipsey was an enigma of some sort because of his knowledge, approach, and style of carrying out his plans which distinguished him from his peers in all respect.

Hussle's strategy towards success can be hinged on a couple of principles you can adapt in your business as an entrepreneur or whatever field you find yourself.

Have a core product: It's important you have something to launch your presence in the market and for Nipsey Hussle that was his music

Segment your fans: By doing this, you will be able to customize your message and offers towards your audience. Nipsey Hussle was able to do this with the $100 mix tape move by knowing fans who truly were raving fans.

Diversify your business/Not putting your eggs in one basket: Basically, always save for a rainy day as things are not always going to run smoothly for you as a business owner, so it's important that you diversify. With Nipsey Hussle did this by investing in a variety of things: Cryptocurrency, Real Estate, etc.

Building a wholesome system.

Strategic partnerships (This includes planning, knowing your value and being deliberate in your moves.) As a business owner, it's important you go into an agreement confidently, and you can only do this by understanding your self-worth as this mindset would prevent you from being at the shorter end of a deal and knowing when to walk or accept a deal. Nipsey Hussle was a real-life example of self-worth and respect combined with a knack for top-notch planning. In an interview he said, he never felt comfortable until he made sure he had planned a process from point A to point B.

"I hope my story inspires everyone out there to keep hustling and chasing their dreams." - Nipsey Hussle

References

The following sites were used as research for this book.

https://blackdoctor.org/too-big-to-fail-nipsey-hussle-brings-stem-to-crenshaw/

https://everydaypower.com/nipsey-hussle-quotes/

https://medium.com/@nathanhastingsspaine/nipsey-was-right-you-can-receive-back-pay-e2d5f8017516

https://medium.com/@nwyatt227/nipsey-hussles-10-steps-to-building-a-music-empire-f6d372d8cfdc

https://spectrumnews1.com/ca/la-west/news/2019/06/05/pushing-nipsey-s-vision-forward

https://spectrumnews1.com/ca/la-west/news/2019/08/15/what-is-the-future-of-nipsey-hussle-s-marathon-store-lot-

https://thegrio.com/2019/04/02/5-brilliant-business-moves-from-nipsey-hussle/

https://thesource.com/2020/03/31/nipsey-from-the-issue-thesource/

https://theundefeated.com/features/nipsey-hussle-puma-partnership-was-strong-and-authentic/

https://twitter.com/ermiasthagreat/status/1120300288055894018

https://vocal.media/beat/25-nipsey-hussle-lyrics

https://www.10news.com/entertainment/nipsey-hussles-family-rejects-fundraising-for-his-kids

https://www.awakenthegreatnesswithin.com/35-inspirational-nipsey-hussle-quotes-on-success/

https://www.billboard.com/articles/columns/hip-hop/7550118/karen-civil-steve-steve-o-carless-marathon-agency

https://www.billboard.com/articles/columns/hip-hop/7840863/nipsey-hussle-marathon-clothing-smart-store

https://www.bitdegree.org/tutorials/follow-coin/

https://www.brainyquote.com/authors/nipsey-hussle-quotes

https://www.entrepreneur.com/article/331766

92

https://www.forbes.com/sites/julianmitchell/2018/03/01/the-art-of-being-self-made-a-conversation-with-nipsey-hussle/#317739a6a07f

https://www.forbes.com/sites/morgansimon/2019/04/11/lessons-in-impact-investing-from-nipsey-hussle/#19cce5e7748e

https://www.forbes.com/sites/morgansimon/2019/04/11/lessons-in-impact-investing-from-nipsey-hussle/#5321a1df748e

https://www.geoblink.com/blog/market-penetration-examples/

https://www.eda.gov/opportunity-zones/

https://www.meon1.com/eng/coaching/nipsey-hussles-top-10-rules-for-success-nipseyhussle/

https://www.nbcnews.com/news/nbcblk/nipsey-hussle-s-commitment-was-his-l-neighborhood-where-he-n989641

https://www.revolt.tv/2019/4/2/20825363/9-inspirational-nipsey-hussle-quotes

https://www.thebmex.com/post/2018/03/02/21-money-lessons-from-nipsey-hussles-victory-lap

https://www.vector90.com

https://www.washingtonpost.com/outlook/2019/04/08/how-nipsey-hussle-inspired-thousands-eritrean-americans/

https://www.xxlmag.com/news/2017/06/nipsey-hussle-launches-marathon-store-los-angeles/

Final Surprise Bonus

Final words from the author...

Hope you've enjoyed this "Nipsey Hussle on Entrepreneurship" book.

It was the utmost privilege performing deep research and bringing forth this information to the public for you to enjoy.

I always like to overdeliver, so I'd like to give you one final bonus.

Do me a favor, if you enjoyed this book, please leave a review on Amazon.

It'll help get the word out so more people can find out more about our beloved superstar as a tribute and homage.

If you do, I'll send you one of my most cherished collection report— Free:

Nipsey Hussle: The Complete Discography Collection From The Beginning to the Very End

A complete list of all of Nipsey's work that was ever published (or not published). As a Nipsey Hussle fan, you'll find this utmost valuable and cannot be missed!

Here's how to claim your free report:

1. Leave a review on the online store where you've purchased this book from (longer the better but I'd be grateful for any length)

2. Send a screenshot to: jjvancebooks@gmail.com

Receive your free report –"**The Complete Discography Collection From The Beginning to the Very End**"–*immediately*!

www.ingramcontent.com/pod-product-compliance
Lightning Source LLC
Chambersburg PA
CBHW061430050726
47593CB00006B/2282